Making Shapes

Jan Anderson

Rigby PM Plus Nonfiction Sapphire Level
Color Around Us
The Science of Cooking
Fibers in Fashion
Making Shapes
Built Like That
Measure for Measure

Rigby PM Plus Nonfiction
part of the Rigby PM Program
Sapphire Level

U.S. edition © 2004 Rigby Education
Harcourt Achieve Inc.
10801 N. MoPac Expressway
Building #3
Austin, TX 78759
www.harcourtachieve.com

Text © 2003 Thomson Learning Australia
Illustrations © 2003 Thomson Learning Australia
Originally published in Australia by Thomson Learning Australia

All rights reserved. No part of this publication may be reproduced or transmitted in any form or by any means, electronic or mechanical, including photocopying, recording, taping, or any information storage and retrieval system, without permission in writing from the publisher.

10 9 8 7 6 5 4 3
07

Making Shapes
    ISBN 0 7578 6953 X

Printed in China by 1010 Printing International Ltd

Acknowledgements:
Photographs by **Australian Picture Library**/ Corbis, p. 30/ James L. Amos, p. 27 right/ Archivo Iconografico, S.A., front cover centre, p. 4 bottom/ Christie's Images, p. 8 top left/ Macduff Everton, p. 27 left/ Kevin Fleming, pp. 6 left, 13 top/ Francoise Gervais, p. 1/ Bob Krist, p. 14 left/ Danny Lehman, p. 23/ Araido de Luca, p. 10/ Tania Midgley, p. 5 top/ Philadelphia Museum of Art, front cover bottom left, p. 19 right/ Royalty-free, p. 16/ Scott T. Smith, p. 12 left/ Paul A. Souders, p. 20/ Vince Streano, p. 14 right/ Stewart Tilger, front cover top right, p. 5 bottom/ Ron Watts, p. 11 left/ Chad Weckler, front cover top left, p. 17/ Nik Wheeler, p. 11 right/ Michael S. Yamashita, p. 6 right; **Getty Images**/ Imagebank, p. 24 bottom/ Stone, p. 21 right/ Taxi, p. 13 bottom; **Image Addict**, front cover bottom right, pp. 12 right, 15 top right, 18 bottom right, 22 left, 22 centre right, 22 centre left, 22 bottom, 28 bottom right, 28 centre right, 29 top left, 29 top right, 29 centre right; **Imagen**/ Bill Thomas, pp. 8 bottom left, 8 bottom right, 9 top left, 9 top right, 9 bottom right; **Kosta Boda**/ Hans Runesson, p. 26; **PhotoDisc**, back cover, pp. 4 centre left, 4 top, 15 bottom left, 15 bottom right, 19 left; **The Picture** Source/ Terry Oakley, pp. 7, 10-11/ James Riser, pp. 18 top, 18 bottom left.

Contents

Chapter 1   Shapes Around Us   4

Chapter 2   Clay   6

Chapter 3   Wood   8

Chapter 4   Wool and Cotton   12

Chapter 5   Rubber   14

Chapter 6   Metals   18

Chapter 7   Glass   24

Chapter 8   Plastics   28

Glossary   32

Index   33

Chapter 1

Shapes Around Us

Everywhere we look, there are objects made in different shapes. A ball is round like a sphere. A coin is shaped like a very flat cylinder. A sculpture, however, has an irregular shape.

How do we make these shapes? What kinds of materials do we use? These are the questions that designers think about every time they design something new.

In the past, most materials — like wood and clay — came from the natural environment. Today designers use manufactured materials, such as metals and plastics. Plastics are the newest kind of material; they are **synthetic**, and are made from chemicals found in oil.

With modern technology, we can shape materials in new and different ways. Designers today have many materials to choose from, and use many processes to shape things.

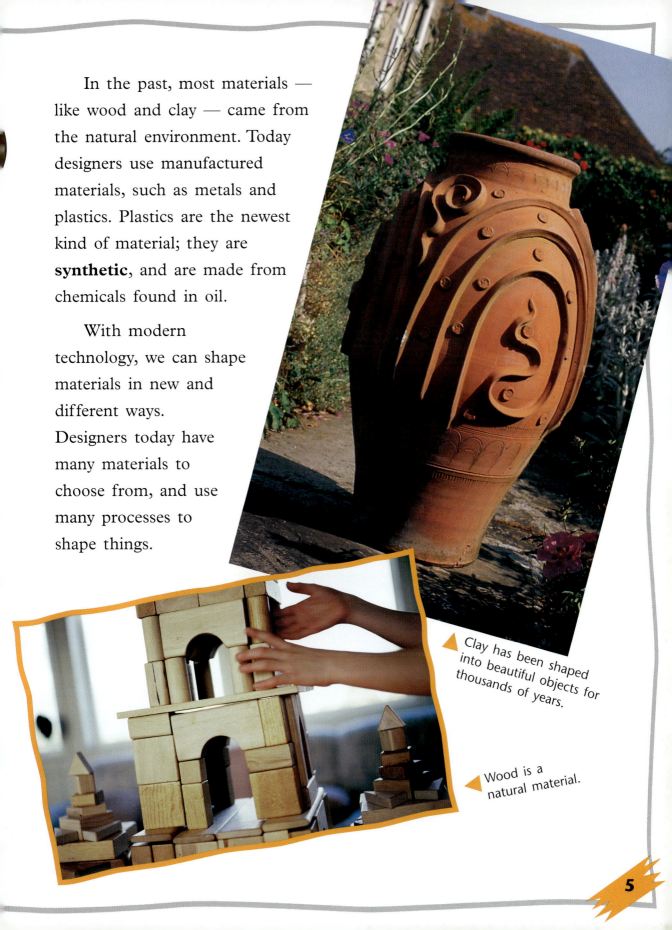

◀ Clay has been shaped into beautiful objects for thousands of years.

◀ Wood is a natural material.

Chapter 2

Clay

Clay is a natural material that people have used for centuries. It is dug out of the ground and can be made into objects like bowls and cups, and even bricks for building houses.

The Potter's Wheel

A bowl or vase begins as a ball of soft clay. The potter centers the ball on a spinning wheel. The hands are used as tools to shape the clay upward or outward.

Objects made on a potter's wheel are **symmetrical**. Although a potter's main tools are his or her hands, sometimes small wooden tools are used to help shape the clay.

◀ First the potter centers the ball of clay. Then he shapes the vase.

Some tools a potter may use. ▼

Making Bricks from Clay

Until the 1950s, bricks were shaped by pressing clay into **molds**. Some bricks are still made this way, but most are made by forcing clay through a **die** that is shaped like a rectangle. A continuous "column" of clay is **extruded**.

The column of clay is cut into individual bricks using wire. The bricks are then baked in a **kiln.**

Chapter 3

Wood

Like clay, wood is a natural material. One of the oldest ways of shaping wood was to carve it.

Wood-turning

Wood-turners work on a machine called a **lathe**. A lathe is very similar to a potter's wheel.

A plain piece of wood is put into the lathe, where it is held firmly. The wood is turned around and around. As it turns, just like the ball of clay on the potter's wheel, the wood-turner shapes the wood.

◀ A plain piece of wood in the lathe — before it is shaped.

The wood takes shape. ▶

Wood is a hard material, and the wood-turner needs metal tools to shape the piece of wood he or she is working on.

Many different shapes can be made on a lathe.

A **chisel** is used to make simple shapes. A **gouger** makes fancy shapes.

Wood-turners wear goggles to protect their eyes from chips of wood flying through the air. Sometimes they wear a mask, so they don't breathe in sawdust.

Bending Wood into Shapes

Bentwood chairs are made by bending wood into shape.

The wood is steamed. This makes the **resin** in the wood soft. The wood becomes **pliable**. It can then be bent around a form, or shape. The curved backs, arms, and legs of the chairs are made in this way.

After bending the wood, it is put aside to let the resin harden once again. The wood keeps its new shape.

The wood is steamed into shape before it is assembled into furniture.

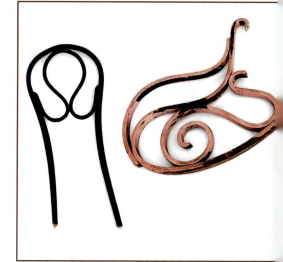

Did you know?

People knew how to steam and bend wood as long ago as the Middle Ages, but it wasn't until Michael Thonet improved this technique in the 1830s, that bentwood chairs could be **mass-produced.**

This kind of chair is very popular in cafés and restaurants around the world.

Chapter 4
Wool and Cotton

Wool and cotton are natural materials. Wool comes from animals such as sheep, goats, and llamas. Cotton comes from plants. Both are **fibers** that can be made into thread and then woven to make shapes.

A llama being shorn

A cotton-picking machine

Weaving is an old craft. In some parts of the world, wool and cotton are still woven by hand into cloth and rugs.

However, these days cloth is usually made in factories on mechanical **looms**.

Traditional hand-weaving

A mechanical loom

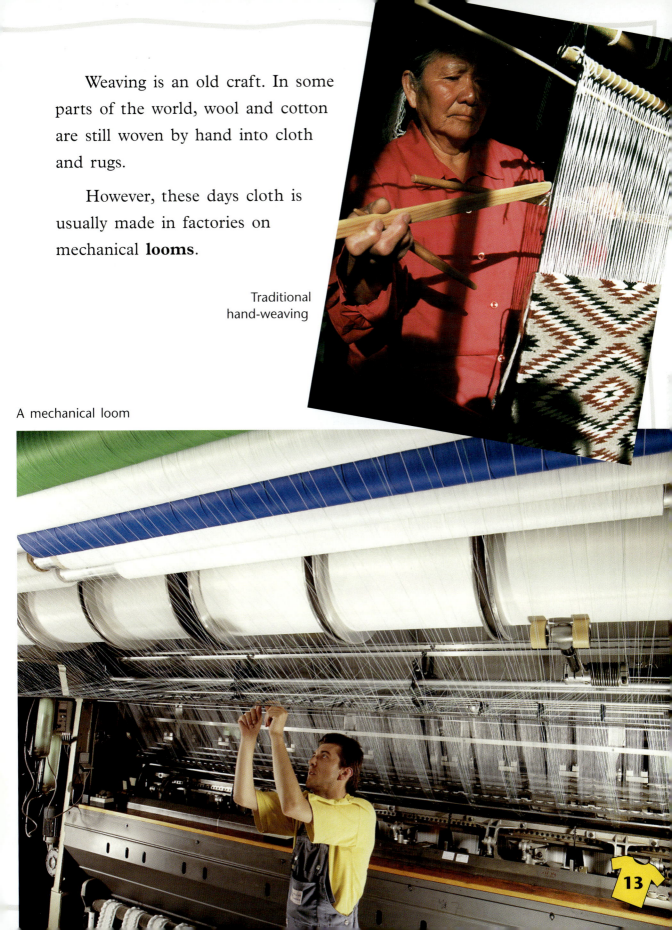

Chapter 5

Rubber

Rubber is a very **versatile** material. It can be shaped into gloves to protect our hands or hot water bottles that keep us warm in bed at night. But most rubber is used to make the tires of cars, trucks, and bicycles.

Most of the rubber that we use comes from the sap of the rubber tree. Some synthetic rubber, however, is made from oil and coal.

Natural rubber is obtained by tapping into the bark of the rubber tree.

Why is rubber a useful material? Rubber stretches well. A wetsuit can be eased over your body.

Rubber is hard to puncture. A glove, or a tire, will not get a hole in it easily.

Rubber stays cool when it's under pressure and has a heavy load on it. This makes it ideal for tires.

Did you know?
Rubber tires are made from a mixture of natural and synthetic rubbers.

Shapes for Safety — the Tread of a Tire

Every tire is made with a **tread**. This is the part of the tire that touches the ground. It has a pattern molded on its surface.

The shape of the tread helps the tire to grip slippery roads. It is dangerous to drive with tires that have worn-out treads because the car cannot grip the road.

Tread
(outer layer of tire)

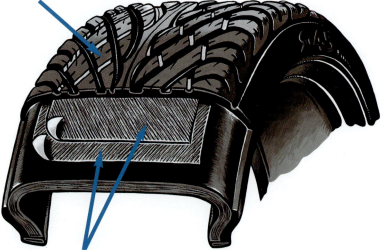

Other layers of the tire

Tires are made with treads of many different shapes to suit different kinds of vehicles and different driving conditions.

How the Tread Is Made

Rubber is fed into a special machine. It is forced through a die, which makes the pattern on the tread. This process is called **extrusion**.

The tread is then cut into the right length for each kind of tire. A truck tire is bigger than a car tire, so the length of tread is longer.

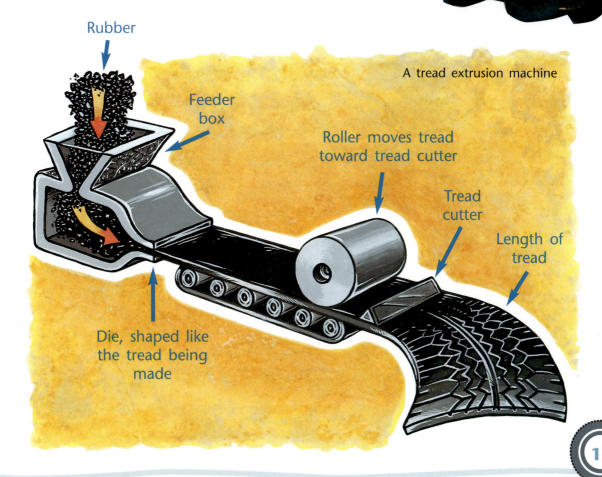

A tread extrusion machine

Rubber
Feeder box
Die, shaped like the tread being made
Roller moves tread toward tread cutter
Tread cutter
Length of tread

Chapter 6

Metals

There are many different ways that we can shape metals into useful or decorative objects.

Copper

Copper was one of the first metals to be manufactured.

Copper can be spun into bowls, plates, and saucepans. A metal spinner is a person who changes a flat circle of metal into a hollow shape, using a lathe. The circle of metal is called a **blank**.

The blank is held firmly in the lathe. As the lathe rotates, the blank is forced over a die that is shaped like the object to be made (such as a bowl). A long steel tool is used to force the blank gradually over the die.

Copper is also shaped into wire that is used to carry electricity around our homes.

Copper blanks

Copper being spun

Copper wire

Copper Alloys

Sometimes copper is combined with other metals, to make **alloys.** A range of methods is used to shape alloys.

The nickel, dime, and quarter are made with an alloy of copper and nickel. They are shaped in a machine called a press.

Blanks shaped like very thin cylinders of the alloy are fed into the press. They are struck on both sides at the same time by two dies.

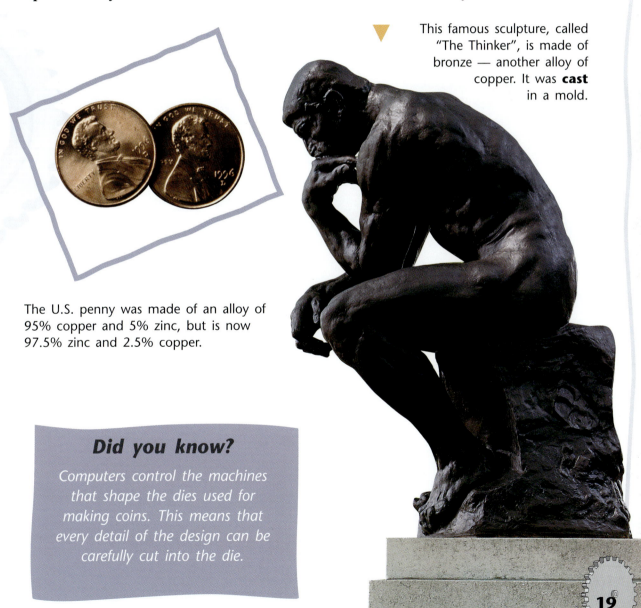

This famous sculpture, called "The Thinker", is made of bronze — another alloy of copper. It was **cast** in a mold.

The U.S. penny was made of an alloy of 95% copper and 5% zinc, but is now 97.5% zinc and 2.5% copper.

Did you know?

Computers control the machines that shape the dies used for making coins. This means that every detail of the design can be carefully cut into the die.

Steel

Steel is a strong metal that has many uses. It is used as beams in buildings for extra support. It is important in cars, trains, railway tracks, and airplanes.

Like other materials, it can be shaped in different ways. It can be cast in molds to make thick slabs of steel. Steel can be rolled into thinner, flat steel. It can be shaped into wire.

Some kinds of flat steel are shaped into roofing material, and other kinds into car bodies.

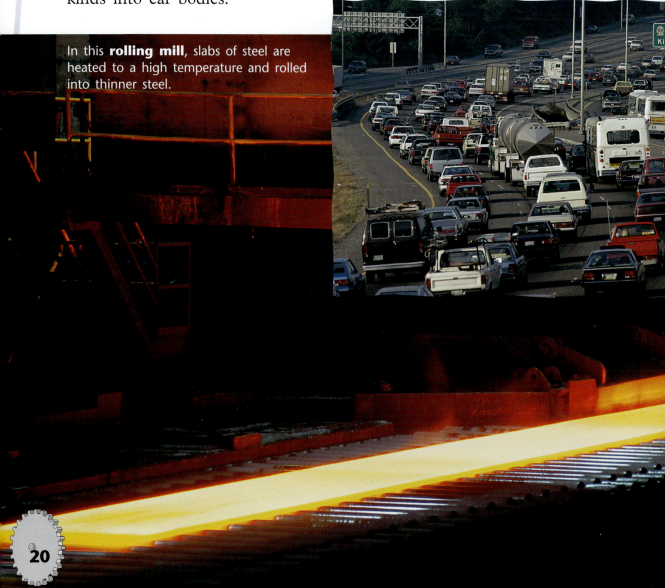

In this **rolling mill**, slabs of steel are heated to a high temperature and rolled into thinner steel.

Shaping Car Bodies

Every day thousands of cars are made around the world, and they have many different shapes. Factories make car bodies from big pieces of flat steel. Steel is used because it is strong and can help protect the passengers inside.

A car body is made in **panels**. Each panel has a different shape, such as a hood, a door, or a roof. All the shapes are assembled to make the body. Robots put the pieces together in the factory.

The shapes are made by machines called **presses**, which stamp the shapes out of the flat steel.

1. A **stamping press** stamps the blank onto a die of the right shape to make a door, roof, or hood panel. It presses the blank down hard onto the die.

2. Robots assemble and **weld** the panels together into a car body.

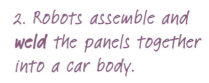

Making Wire

Steel wire is used to make fences, nails, staples, pins, and strong steel rope. The wire is made by pulling a rod of steel through a series of dies with smaller and smaller holes. This makes the wire thinner and thinner (and longer).

This is done in a place called a wire mill.

Staples

Barbed wire

Safety pins

A wire mill

Chapter 7

Glass

Imagine a world without glass. There would be no windows, telescopes, or microscopes. There would be no glass fibers for carrying telephone messages, or the Internet.

Glass is made from a natural resource — sand.

Glass fibres

Glass for Windows

In the past, one way of making sheets of glass was to pull **molten** glass out between rollers. However, this glass was uneven in thickness, and needed grinding and polishing to make it smooth.

In the 1950s, an Englishman named Alastair Pilkington developed the "float" process. In this process, molten glass from a **furnace** flows onto a "lake" of molten tin. It spreads out to make glass of even thickness. Glass made in this way is very smooth because the molten tin is smooth.

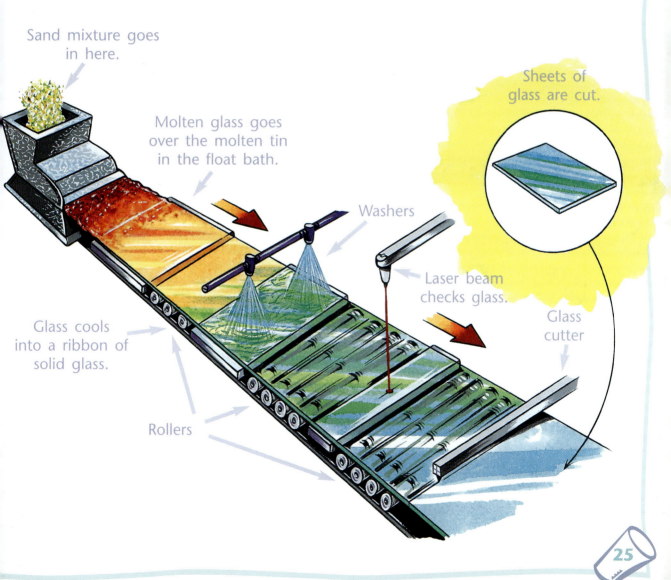

Blowpipe ▼

Working with Glass

Glass-blowing is an old way of working with glass. Glass-blowers work with molten glass at white-hot temperatures to mold it into shapes such as vases and bowls.

A glass-blower dips a long metal pipe, called a blowpipe, into a furnace containing liquid glass. Out comes a lump of molten glass.

Then the glass-blower starts turning the blowpipe, shaping the glass while rotating the pipe. As the pipe is turned, the glass-blower blows down its center to hollow out the piece of glass.

Glass-blowers must be strong and able to work in a hot environment as they need to work near the furnace.

A glass-blower needs:

- Good lungs for blowing out the glass through the hollow blowpipe.

- Hands, and a wad of wet newspaper which is held against the blob of hot glass to mold it into a spherical shape.

- A flat piece of wood that has been soaked in water. This is used to flatten the base of the glass object, such as a vase.

- Steel tongs to help shape parts of the glass — like the neck of a vase. These tongs are also used to hollow out the inside of the object being made.

Did you know?

Glass-blowing is an ancient craft. The Romans invented the first glass-blowing pipe over 2000 years ago.
They used a hollow tube of iron.

Chapter 8

Plastics

From plastic toys and telephones, to plastic cups and canoes — plastic has changed our lives forever.

Plastic, which is a synthetic material, is the "wonder material" of today. Different kinds of plastic are made from chemicals that come from oil. Since the 1950s, plastics have been used to make many different objects.

Why Plastics Are So Useful

- They melt at low temperatures, which makes them easy to mold.
- They can be molded into almost any shape.
- They can be colored or transparent.
- They can be hard, soft, flexible, rigid, or even made like a foam that has set.
- They are lightweight, strong, and waterproof.

This toy was molded into shape.

A cooler made of a kind of "foam" plastic is light to carry, and a good **insulator**.

Most buckets are now made of plastic, rather than metal. Plastic is strong and waterproof. It is lighter than metal and can be made in bright colors.

Blow Molding

Plastic bottles and jars are made by blow molding.

A piece of molten plastic is poured into a mold that is shaped like a bottle. Hot air is blown into the plastic, which expands to fill the shape of the mold. A bottle is formed.

When the plastic is cool, the mold is opened, and the bottle drops out.

The mold is in two pieces. It is closed, and plastic is poured in.

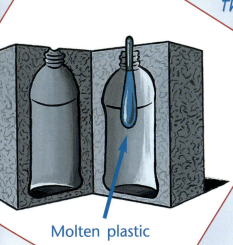

Molten plastic

Pipe

The hot air is blown through the pipe into the plastic.

The bottle is dropped out of the mold.

Did you know?
If you look closely at a plastic bottle, you will see two vertical lines, or ridges of plastic, on opposite sides of the bottle. This is where the two halves of the mold met.

29

Injection Molding

Many plastic shapes, such as flower pots and videotape cases, are made by a process called **injection molding**.

1 Granules of colored plastic (A) are fed into the molding machine.

2 A screw, or plunger (B), pushes the plastic granules into a heated chamber (C), where they melt.

3 The liquid plastic (D) is then forced into a mold (E) shaped like the object that is to be made — for example, a flower pot.

4 The plastic cools almost immediately and the shape sets solid.

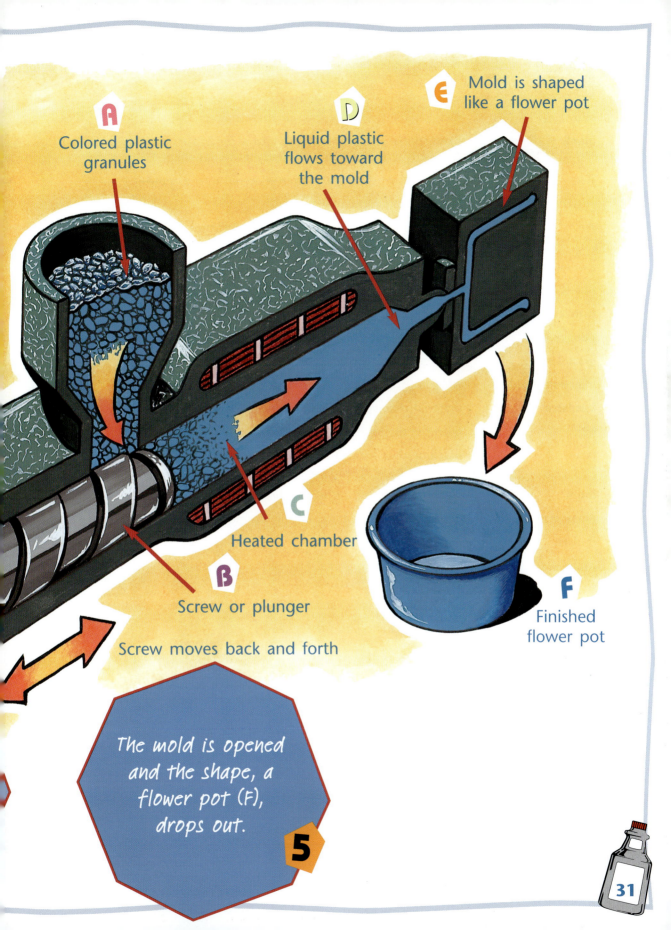

Glossary

alloy	metal made by mixing two or more metals
blank	plain, flat piece of metal, cut into a particular shape and size, ready to be made into a three-dimensional shape (with a die)
cast	to shape by pouring a molten material into a mold
chisel	tool for shaping wood
die	a two-dimensional or three-dimensional tool for making a particular shape. A mold is a three-dimensional die.
extrusion (extruded)	forcing a material through a die that is two-dimensional
fibers	very thin threads, from plants or animals, or made of plastic or glass
furnace	very hot oven used for melting a material
gouger	tool for shaping wood
granules	small spherical particles of a material
injection molding	when a molten material is forced into a mold
insulator	material that keeps out heat or cold
kiln	oven for drying products, like pots, bricks or even timber
lathe	machine that rotates a piece of material (like wood or metal) so you can shape it with tools
loom	machine or frame on which threads are woven
mass-produced	made in large numbers, usually by machines
molten	melted
mold	a three-dimensional die. Molds are used for making three-dimensional shapes.
panels	pieces of material that are part of a bigger shape, or object
pliable	able to be bent without breaking
press	machine for cutting or forcing a material into a particular shape
resin	kind of glue
rolling mill	place where a thick material is flattened by rollers to make it thinner
stamping press	press for making blanks into three-dimensional shapes
symmetrical	when one half of an object is the exact opposite shape to the other half
synthetic	human-made
tread	part of a tire that touches the road
versatile	can do or be used for different things
weld	join two pieces of metal